debbie macomber

Debbie Macomber's highly successful Cedar Cove series continues to delight her fans with its carefully crafted stories of love and friendship. With more than 60 million copies of Debbie's books in print, her compelling characters have touched hearts all over the world.

Debbie's marvelous books aren't the only way she shares her talent with others. Debbie is an avid knitter who believes strongly in "giving back" to her community. One way she accomplishes this is by drawing attention to worthy causes through her books.

While working on her popular novel, **The Shop on Blossom Street**, Debbie learned about an organization called *Warm Up America!* This charity group consists of knitters and crocheters who create 7" x 9" blocks which are joined into blankets for the needy. Debbie became one of the first board members for Warm Up America!, and she continues to work tirelessly on its behalf. Debbie urges everyone who uses these patterns to take a few minutes to knit or crochet a block for this cause. On page 38, you will find out how, with just a little bit of yarn, you can make a real difference.

Debbie also hopes that **this collection of ten fun and stylish fashions** will inspire you to discover the rich rewards of knitting for yourself and those you love.

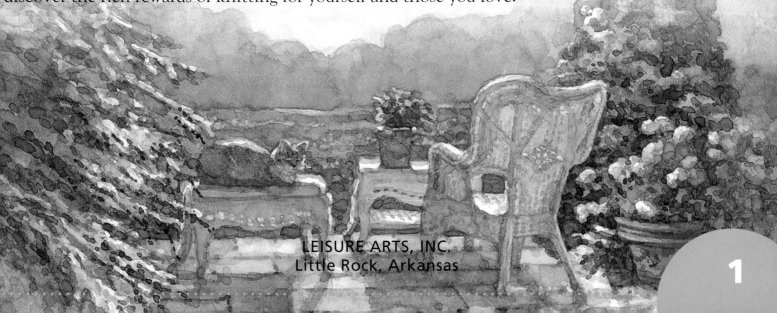

LEISURE ARTS, INC.
Little Rock, Arkansas

1

a word from
LEISURE ARTS
and MIRA books

Read The Books that Inspired the Projects

knit along with
DEBBIE MACOMBER

As many of Debbie Macomber's fans know, the fascinating characters in her stories are often knitters who create thoughtful gifts for their loved ones. To help you experience the rewards of knitting just like your favorite Cedar Cove citizens, Leisure Arts is excited to offer this companion publication to the popular book series. *Knit Along with Debbie Macomber—The Cedar Cove Collection* is filled with knitting patterns inspired by the stories.

You'll discover excerpts from Debbie's books and enjoy four delicious recipes contributed by Debbie and her readers. Also included are patterns for four sample blocks that you can make to contribute to Debbie's favorite nonprofit organization, *Warm Up America!*

For more knitting fun with Debbie, look for these Leisure Arts instruction books: *Knit Along with Debbie Macomber—The Shop on Blossom Street* and *Knit Along with Debbie Macomber—A Good Yarn.*

Read all of Debbie's heartwarming stories, then knit up a little creativity from Leisure Arts.

LOOK FOR DEBBIE'S HEARTWARMING STORIES AT BOOKSTORES EVERYWHERE, AND COLLECT ALL THREE KNITTING PUBLICATIONS INSPIRED BY HER CEDAR COVE AND BLOSSOM STREET NOVELS.

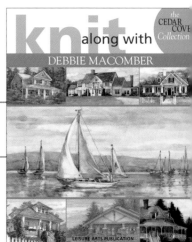

Leaflet# 4658

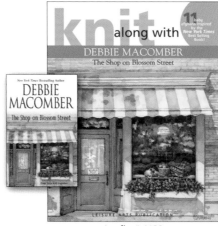

Leaflet# 4132

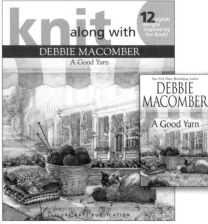

Leaflet# 4135

To find out more about Debbie Macomber, visit www.debbiemacomber.com or www.mirabooks.com

For information about these and other Leisure Arts publications call 1.800.526.5111 or visit www.leisurearts.com

LEISURE ARTS
the art of everyday living

2

letters from Cedar Cove

If you haven't already met the interesting people who live in Cedar Cove, then you'll surely want to take a peek at these letters. They were written by some of the fascinating characters who populate Debbie's imaginary town. Each letter highlights a particular book in the series. We're sharing the letters in the order of each book's release, beginning with the delightful novel that started it all, 16 Lighthouse Road.

16 Lighthouse Road

Olivia Lockhart
16 Lighthouse Road
Cedar Cove, Washington

Dear Reader,

I'm inviting you to my home and my town of Cedar Cove because I want you to meet my family, friends and neighbors. Come and hear their stories — maybe even their secrets!

I have to admit that my own secrets are pretty open. My marriage failed some years ago, and I have a rather...difficult relationship with my daughter, Justine. Then there's my mother, Charlotte, who has plenty of opinions and is always willing to share them.

Here's an example: I'm a family court judge and she likes to drop in on my courtroom. Recently I was hearing a divorce petition. In Charlotte's view, young Cecilia and Ian Randall hadn't tried hard enough to make their marriage work — and I agreed. So I rendered my judgment: Divorce Denied.

Well, you wouldn't believe the reaction! Thanks to an article by Jack Griffin, the editor of our local paper (and a man I wouldn't mind seeing more of!), everyone's talking.

Cedar Cove — people love it and sometimes they leave it, but they never forget it!

See you soon...
Olivia

Grace Sherman
204 Rosewood Lane
Cedar Cove, Washington

Dear Reader,

If you've been to Cedar Cove before we've probably met. You can usually find me either at home or at the public library, where I work. I've lived in this town all my life and raised two daughters here. But my husband and I—well, about six months ago, he just disappeared. Where's Dan? Why did he go? Who's he with? Will I ever find out?

My hometown, my family and friends, bring me comfort during this difficult time. I'm continually reminded that life goes on. Justine—the only daughter of my best friend, Olivia Lockhart—impulsively got married a little while ago. My own daughter Kelly recently had a baby. Unfortunately, she refuses to accept that Dan might not return to see his first grandchild. My older daughter, Maryellen, is more realistic. I think she's seeing a new man, but for some reason she won't tell me who it is.

Then there's Jack, who's been pursuing a romance with Olivia, and his son Eric, and Eric's girlfriend, Shelly (I think she's pregnant), and Zach and Rosemary Cox, whose marriage is reputedly on the skids and. . . Well, just come on over and we'll talk!

Grace

Rosie Cox
311 Pelican Court
Cedar Cove, Washington

Dear Reader,

One thing about Cedar Cove—people sure are interested in what other people are doing. Take me, for instance. Everybody in this town knows that my husband, Zach, and I recently got a divorce. Everybody also knows that Judge Olivia Lockhart decreed a pretty unusual custody arrangement. It won't be the kids moving between my place and Zach's. We're the ones who'll be going back and forth!

Olivia isn't immune to gossip herself. Will she stay with Jack, the guy who runs our local paper, or will she get back with her ex? Inquiring minds want to know!

But the really big gossip has to do with the dead guy—the man who died at a local bed-and-breakfast. Who is he and why did he show up there in the middle of the night? Roy McAfee, our local private investigator, is absolutely determined to find out. I hope he does—and then I'll let you know! See you soon...

Rosie

44 Cranberry Point

PEGGY BELDON
THYME AND TIDE B AND B
44 CRANBERRY POINT
CEDAR COVE, WASHINGTON

Dear Reader,

I love living in Cedar Cove, but things haven't been the same since a man died in our B and B. Turns out his name was Max Russell, and Bob had known him briefly in Vietnam. We still don't have any idea why he came here and—most important of all—who killed him. Because now it appears that he was poisoned.

Not that we're providing the only news in Cedar Cove these days. I heard that Jon Bowman and Maryellen Sherman are getting married. And Maryellen's mom, Grace, has more than her share of interested men! The question is: Which one is she going to choose? Olivia is back from her honeymoon, and her mother, Charlotte (who's in her mid-seventies at least), seems to have a man in her life, too. I'm not sure Olivia's too pleased....

There's lots of other gossip I could tell you. Come by for a cup of tea and one of my blueberry muffins and we'll talk.

Peggy

50 Harbor Street

Corrie McAfee
50 Harbor Street
Cedar Cove, Washington

Dear Reader,

Considering that I'm married to Cedar Cove's private investigator, you might think I enjoy mysteries. But I don't—especially when they involve us! Roy's been receiving anonymous postcards and messages asking if we "regret the past." We don't know what they mean....

On a more positive note, we're both delighted that our daughter, Linnette, has moved to Cedar Cove to work at the new medical clinic. A while ago I attended the humane society's "Dog and Bachelor Auction," where I bought her a date with Cal Washburn, who works at Cliff Harding's horse farm. Unfortunately, Linnette is less enthusiastic about this date than I am.

Speaking of Cliff, the romance between him and Grace Sherman is back on. But that's only one of the many interesting stories here in Cedar Cove. So why don't you stop by for coffee and I'll tell you everything that's new!

Corrie

6 Rainier Drive

Justine Gunderson
6 Rainier Drive
Cedar Cove, Washington

Dear Reader,

As you may have heard, we've recently had quite a shock. My husband, Seth, and I lost our business, The Lighthouse restaurant—to arson. The investigation continues. The prime suspect is a young ex-employee named Anson Butler, who disappeared right after the fire.

So Seth and I are trying to sort out our lives. (And let me tell you, this kind of crisis is not good for a marriage.) In the meantime, life goes on for everyone else in Cedar Cove—with marriages, births, reunions and even the occasional scandal. One of the most interesting pieces of news is that Cal, who works on Cliff Harding's ranch, is now rescuing wild mustangs from Wyoming.

I have to run—I'm meeting an old friend, Warren Saget, for lunch. Let's talk soon, and I'll fill you in on everything that's happening in town!

Justine

scarf exchange

When the city council voted against building a health clinic, Charlotte's knitting group joined her in a public protest. Unfortunately, the retirees forgot to get a permit for their demonstration. Charlotte's friend, Laura, says she's looking forward to being incarcerated — she'll be able to catch up on her knitting! In the meantime, the ladies are planning a scarf exchange to keep their minds off their upcoming court date.

■□□□ BEGINNER

Finished Size: 7" x 60" to 63"
(18 cm x 152.5 cm to 160 cm)

MATERIALS
All Scarves made with Bulky Weight Yarn 🔳5 BULKY

1. Solid Scarf
[1.76 ounces, 55 yards
(50 grams, 50 meters) per ball]:
Red Speckled - 2 balls

2. Solid Scarf
[1.76 ounces, 82 yards
(50 grams, 75 meters) per ball]:
Green - 2 balls

3. Solid Scarf
[1.76 ounces, 55 yards
(50 grams, 50 meters) per ball]:
Blue Speckled - 2 balls

4. Random Stripe Scarf
[1.76 ounces, 82 yards
(50 grams, 75 meters) per skein]:
Blue - 2 skeins
Red - 1 skein

5. Even Stripe Scarf
[6 ounces, 185 yards
(170 grams, 169 meters) per skein]:
Red - 1 skein
Black - 1 skein

6. Even Stripe Scarf
[1.76 ounces, 55 yards
(50 grams, 50 meters) per ball]:
Black Speckled - 2 balls
Red Speckled - 1 ball
[1.76 ounces, 82 yards
(50 grams, 75 meters) per ball]:
Red - 1 ball

7. Progressive Stripe Scarf
Bulky Weight Yarn
[6 ounces, 185 yards
(170 grams, 169 meters) per skein]:
Green - 1 skein
Blue - 1 skein
Straight knitting needles, size 13 (9 mm) **or**
size needed for gauge
Yarn needle

GAUGE: In Garter Stitch (knit every row),
17 sts = 7" (17.75 cm);
16 rows = 4" (10 cm)

The four Scarves given are basically the same Scarf. What makes them different is the stripe sequence. You can choose your favorite colors, mix and match yarns in the same weight, and make stripes as you desire. Create a Scarf that fits your personality or one that would make the perfect gift.

Instructions begin on page 10.

"Laura and I are going to take a trip out to the Silverdale yarn store this afternoon," Charlotte said. She needed more yarn about as much as the desert needed more sand, but Olivia didn't say so. If buying yarn of every weight and color made her mother happy, Olivia could only approve.

—from *204 Rosewood Lane*

charlotte's
kitchen cozies

Charlotte Jefferson is Cedar Cove's ultimate recipe collector. She says the best dishes are served at wakes, and since she attends funerals pretty regularly these days, she's going to have to get another index card box for all the recipes she's picked up. Charlotte also attends a weekly potluck at the senior citizen center. Transporting all those casseroles and baked goods requires plenty of hot pads and pot holders, so Charlotte uses these quick knitting patterns to keep a selection handy.

◼◼◻◻ **EASY**

Finished Sizes: Pot Holder - 7½" x 9½"
 (19 cm x 24 cm)
 Hot Pad - 9½" (24 cm) square

Note: Instructions are written for the Pot Holder, with the Hot Pad in braces { }. If only one number is given, it applies to both projects.

MATERIALS
 Medium Weight Cotton Yarn **4** MEDIUM
 [2.5 ounces (70.9 grams) per ball]:
 Solid - 2 balls
 [2 ounces (56.7 grams) per ball]:
 Multi - 2 balls
 Straight knitting needles, size 7 (4.5 mm) **or**
 size needed for gauge
 Yarn needle

GAUGE: In Stockinette Stitch, 5 sts = 1" (2.5 cm)

BODY (Make 2)
Using solid color for one side and multicolor for the second side, cast on 38{48} sts.

Row 1: (K1, P1) across.

Row 2 (Right side): (P1, K1) across.

Row 3: (K1, P1) across.

Row 4: (P1, K1) across.

Row 5: K1, P1, K1, P3, (K1, P1) 3 times, ★ K2, P2, (K1, P1) 3 times; repeat from ★ across to last 6 sts, K3, P1, K1, P1.

Row 6: (P1, K1) twice, ★ P3, (K1, P1) twice, K3; repeat from ★ across to last 4 sts, (P1, K1) twice.

Row 7: K1, P1, K1, P5, K1, P1, (K4, P4, K1, P1) across to last 8 sts, K5, P1, K1, P1.

Row 8: (P1, K1) twice, (P5, K5) across to last 4 sts, (P1, K1) twice.

Row 9: K1, P1, K1, P6, (K5, P5) across to last 9 sts, K6, P1, K1, P1.

Row 10: P1, K1, P1, K2, P4, K4, (P1, K1, P4, K4) across to last 5 sts, P2, K1, P1, K1.

Row 11: K1, P1, K1, P2, K1, P3, K3, P1, (K1, P1, K1, P3, K3, P1) across to last 5 sts, K2, P1, K1, P1.

Row 12: P1, K1, P1, K2, P1, K1, P2, K2, ★ (P1, K1) 3 times, P2, K2; repeat from ★ across to last 7 sts, P1, K1, P2, K1, P1, K1.

Row 13: K1, P1, K1, P2, (K1, P1) across to last 5 sts, K2, P1, K1, P1.

Row 14: P1, K1, P1, K2, (P1, K1) across to last 5 sts, P2, K1, P1, K1.

Instructions continued on page 10.

Thursday afternoon was the monthly potluck at the Jackson Senior Center. Charlotte wouldn't have missed it for the world. She arrived early and secured a table for her knitting friends.
—from
16 Lighthouse Road

Row 15: K1, P1, K1, P2, K1, P1, K2, P2, ★ (K1, P1) 3 times, K2, P2; repeat from ★ across to last 7 sts, K1, P1, K2, P1, K1, P1.

Row 16: P1, K1, P1, K2, P1, K3, P3, ★ (K1, P1) twice, K3, P3; repeat from ★ across to last 6 sts, K1, P2, K1, P1, K1.

Row 17: K1, P1, K1, P2, K4, P4, (K1, P1, K4, P4) across to last 5 sts, K2, P1, K1, P1.

Row 18: P1, K1, P1, K6, (P5, K5) across to last 9 sts, P6, K1, P1, K1.

Row 19: (K1, P1) twice, (K5, P5) across to last 4 sts, (K1, P1) twice.

Row 20: P1, K1, P1, K5, P1, K1, (P4, K4, P1, K1) across to last 8 sts, P5, K1, P1, K1.

Row 21: (K1, P1) twice, ★ K3, (P1, K1) twice, P3; repeat from ★ across to last 4 sts, (K1, P1) twice.

Row 22: P1, K1, P1, K3, (P1, K1) 3 times, ★ P2, K2, (P1, K1) 3 times; repeat from ★ across to last 6 sts, P3, K1, P1, K1.

Row 23: (K1, P1) across.

Rows 24-63: Repeat Rows 4-23 twice.

Row 64: (P1, K1) across.

Row 65: (K1, P1) across.

Bind off all sts in pattern.

With **wrong** sides together, sew pieces together.

Designs by Linda Luder.

scarf exhange
continued

SOLID SCARF
Cast on 17 sts.

Knit every row (this is known as Garter Stitch), until Scarf measures approximately 62" (157.5 cm) or until you nearly run out of yarn.

Bind off all sts in **knit**.

Weave in the yarn ends.

EVEN STRIPE SCARF

With Black, cast on 17 sts.

Continuing with Black, knit 24 rows (Garter Stitch).

Tip: When changing colors, cut the yarn leaving a long enough end to be woven in later. Leaving a long end of the new yarn, tie the two colors in a loose knot (close to the last stitch) that you can undo later.

Knit 24 rows with Red; then cut Red and tie on Black.

Continue knitting 24 rows with each color until Scarf measures approximately 60" (152.5 cm) or the length you want.

Bind off all stitches in **knit**.

Go back and untie the knots and hide all the yarn ends on the wrong side by weaving them through the stitches. This will ensure that the knots won't come untied in the future and make your lovely Scarf become a mass of unraveled stitches!

RANDOM STRIPE SCARF

Cast on 17 sts.

Knit every row (Garter Stitch) and change colors as desired, using same method as Even Stripe Scarf and changing colors at the same edge to avoid a line of color within the Garter ridge, until Scarf measures approximately 62" (157.5 cm) or the length you want.

Bind off all stitches in **knit**.

Weave in yarn ends same as Even Stripe Scarf.

PROGRESSIVE STRIPE SCARF

With Blue, cast on 17 sts.

Continuing with Blue, knit every row (Garter Stitch) for 7" (18 cm); do **not** cut Blue.

Tip: When changing colors to work a stripe of 6 rows or less, do **not** cut the yarn. It will be carried along the edge of the Scarf. Leaving a long enough end of the new yarn to be woven in later, tie the two colors in a loose knot (close to the last stitch) that you can undo later.

After working 2 rows, twist the two yarns once to anchor the carried yarn and prevent unsightly loops at the edge of your Scarf.

Knit 4 rows with Green; then cut Green leaving a long end to be woven in later and tie on Blue.

Knit every row with Blue for 5" (12.5 cm); do **not** cut Blue, tie on Green.

Continue to knit every row, working in the following stripe sequence:

6 rows Green
3" (7.5 cm) Blue
4" (10 cm) Green
6 rows Blue
5" (12.5 cm) Green
6 rows Blue
7" (18 cm) Green
4 rows Blue
5" (12.5 cm) Green
6 rows Blue
4" (10 cm) Green
6 rows Blue
5" (12.5 cm) Green
6 rows Blue
7" (18 cm) Green

Bind off all sts in **knit**.

Weave in yarn ends same as Even Stripe Scarf.

chemo turban

One of the best things about knitting is that it gives you a chance to help someone else. By donating a selection of turbans to the nearest cancer treatment center, the Senior Center knitters help the patients feel more comfortable with the changes they're going through. And it makes the knitters feel pretty good, too. Of course, the fashionable cap can also be worn simply because it looks great.

■■□□ EASY

Hat Size: One size fits most adult women.
Finished Size: 22" (56 cm) circumference and 8" (20.5 cm) from edge to top of crown.

Tip: Fit is extremely important. If it is either too tight or too loose it will slide off. You may make a slightly smaller or larger size by changing needle size to obtain a tighter or looser gauge and by changing the length of the Band, which forms the circumference of the Turban.

MATERIALS
Super Bulky Weight Yarn   SUPER BULKY **6**
    [100 yards (91.4 meters) per skein]:
        1 skein
Straight knitting needles, size 9 (5.5 mm) **or**
        size needed for gauge
Yarn needle
T-pins

GAUGE: In Stockinette Stitch,
        10 sts = 4" (10 cm)

Note: This Turban is made in two pieces and stitched together.

BAND
Cast on 10 sts.

Beginning with a **knit** row, work in Stockinette Stitch (knit one row, purl one row) until piece measures 20" (51 cm) from cast on edge **or** desired circumference around head.

Bind off all sts in pattern.

CROWN
Cast on 5 sts.

Row 1 (Right side)**:** K1, (P1, K1) twice.

Note: Mark Row 1 as **right** side.

Row 2: P1, (K1, P1) twice.

Rows 3-10 (Tab)**:** Repeat Rows 1 and 2, 4 times.

Row 11 (Increase row)**:** Purl and knit in first st *(see Purl/Knit Combination Increase, page 44)*, P1, K1, P1, knit and purl in last st *(Fig. 8, page 44)*: 7 sts.

Row 12: K1, (P1, K1) across.

Row 13 (Increase row)**:** Knit and purl in first st, K1, (P1, K1) across to last st, purl and knit in last st: 9 sts.

Row 14: P1, (K1, P1) across.

Row 15 (Increase row)**:** Purl and knit in first st, P1, (K1, P1) across to last st, knit and purl in last st: 11 sts.

Rows 16-23: Repeat Rows 12-15 twice: 19 sts.

Row 24: K1, (P1, K1) across.

Row 25: P1, (K1, P1) across.

Rows 26-29: Repeat Rows 24 and 25 twice.

Rows 30-32: Repeat Rows 12-14: 21 sts.

Rows 33-36: Repeat Rows 24 and 25 twice.

Row 37 (Begin decrease rows)**:** P2 tog *(Fig. 13, page 45)*, K1, (P1, K1) across to last 2 sts, P2 tog: 19 sts.

Row 38: K1, (P1, K1) across.

Row 39: K2 tog *(Fig. 9, page 44)*, P1, (K1, P1) across to last 2 sts, K2 tog: 17 sts.

Row 40: P1, (K1, P1) across.

Row 41: P2 tog, K1, P2 tog, K2 tog, P3 tog *(Fig. 15, page 46)*, K2 tog, P2 tog, K1, P2 tog: 9 sts.

Row 42: K1, (P1, K1) across.

Row 43: K2 tog, P1, K3 tog *(Fig. 10, page 44)*, P1, K2 tog: 5 sts.

Row 44: P1, (K1, P1) twice.

Row 45: P2 tog, K1, P2 tog: 3 sts.

Bind off remaining sts in pattern.

ASSEMBLY

Fold Band in half with **right** side together; whipstitch the cast on and bound off edges together, forming a ring *(Fig. 17, page 46)*.

With **right** side of both pieces facing you, center the Crown tab over the Band seam, lining up cast on edge of the Crown even with the bottom edge of the Band *(Fig. 1)*.

Fig. 1

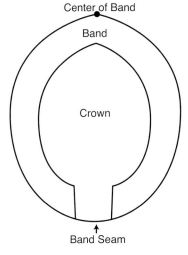

Beginning at inside edge of Band, use a blind stitch to sew the first side of the tab to the Band; whipstitch the cast on edge of the tab to the bottom edge of the Band; blind stitch the remaining side of the tab to the Band; do **not** cut yarn.

Fold the Band in half to find the center point; pin the bind off edge of the Crown to the inside center point on the Band. With **wrong** sides facing you, whipstitch the Crown to the Band, easing the pieces together.

Design by Peggy Schultz.

13

felted knitting tote

For any group of knitters, there's one pattern that seems to define their common interest. And for the ladies who meet at the Jackson Senior Center, that special knit design is this felted knitting tote. It's just as lovely as it is useful, and so roomy that you could use it to carry enough yarn for an afghan.

◼◼◻◻ **EASY**

Finished Size: 16½" wide x 13½" high
(42 cm x 34.5 cm)

MATERIALS

Medium Weight Yarn **4** MEDIUM
[3½ ounces, 223 yards
(100 grams, 204 meters) per ball]:
Green - 4 balls
White - 1 ball
Pink - 1 ball
Straight knitting needles, size 10½ (6.5 mm)
or size needed for gauge
Yarn needle
Plastic rigid foam board for blocking

Felting is a lot of **fun** – when you do it on purpose! Felting is simple. You start with a large, wool-based knitted project. You put it in hot water in your washing machine. And, the project shrinks. You end up with felted knits with a strong, dense, and slightly fuzzy texture, making them perfectly **fabulous** for purses and knitting totes.

Tips for Successful Felting

Because felting is not an exact science, the results are as individual as your knitting. In choosing your yarn, first, read the label. Avoid "superwash" yarns as they are made, specifically, to NOT shrink. Choose a yarn that is at least 50% wool. Novelty yarns used as "carry along" yarn that can be washed in hot water can give great results. Just knit them as a second strand with the main yarn that does felt so they will be pulled into shape.

ALWAYS make a test swatch with all of your yarns and colors to: Check knit gauge, see how the yarn felts, make sure all the yarns in the project felt the way you want them to, and to make sure the colors do not run.

Measure your swatch BEFORE and AFTER you felt it. While this is no guarantee of the final results, it will give you an idea of how this yarn shrinks.

Hold 2 strands of yarn together throughout.

GAUGE: In Stockinette Stitch,
20 sts and 28 rows = 6" (15.25 cm)

The Body will measure 21½" wide x 22½" high (54.5 cm x 57 cm) before felting. The felting process will shrink your Tote more in the length than it does in the width.

BODY (Make 2)

With Green, cast on 71 sts.

Beginning with a **knit** row, work in Stockinette Stitch (knit one row, purl one row) for 38 rows.

Work even in the following color sequence: 3 Rows White, 2 rows **each** of Green, White, (Pink, White) twice, 8 rows Pink, 2 rows **each** of (White, Pink) 3 times, 3 rows White.

Using Green, work even for 20 rows.

Handle: K 28, bind off next 15 sts, knit across: 28 sts **each** side.

Next Row: Purl across to bound off sts; **turn**, add on 15 sts **(Figs. 5a & b, page 43)**, **turn**; purl across: 71 sts.

Work even for 7 rows.

Bind off all sts in **purl**.

FINISHING
ASSEMBLY

With **wrong** sides together, whipstitch Body together along bottom edge **(Fig. 17, page 46)**. Beginning at top edge, weave Body together along one side, matching stripes and ending 2" (5 cm) from bottom edge. Bring bottom seam to meet side seam, forming a "T" shape; whipstitch this edge together.
Repeat for second side.
Turn Tote right side out and tack bottom flaps in place.

Felt Tote **(see Felting, page 47)**.

Design by Peggy Schultz.

Charlotte picked up her knitting bag, which was twice as large as her not insignificant purse, and rested it on her knees. She enjoyed sitting in Olivia's courtroom from time to time. She claimed she got her best knitting done while listening to Olivia's cases.
—from
204 Rosewood Lane

tom's lap robe

Cedar Cove is the kind of place where folks enjoy getting to know their neighbors. Even out-of-town arrivals at the local nursing home are likely to get a visit from volunteers. That's how Charlotte met Tom Harding, a friendly but frail gentleman whose surprising past would soon be revealed.

■■■◻ INTERMEDIATE

Finished Size: 36" x 50" (91.5 cm x 127 cm)

MATERIALS
Bulky Weight Yarn 🏷 **5** BULKY
[6 ounces, 185 yards
(170 grams, 169 meters) per skein]:
Green - 2 skeins
Variegated - 2 skeins
Yellow - 2 skeins
24" (61 cm) or longer circular knitting needle,
size 11 (8 mm) **or** size needed for gauge

GAUGE: In pattern, one repeat (13 sts)
and 15 rows (point to dip) =
4" (10 cm)

Gauge Swatch: 8" x 4" (20.25 cm x 10 cm)
With Green, cast on 26 sts.
Work same as Lap Robe for 15 rows.
Bind off all sts in **knit**.

STRIPE SEQUENCE
★ 5 Rows **each** of Green, Variegated, Yellow;
repeat from ★ for stripe sequence.

Tip: This ripple pattern is a 10 row repeat,
working 5 rows with one color. This avoids
having yarn ends only on one side of the
afghan, and eliminates some of the bulk.

LAP ROBE
With Green, cast on 117 sts.

Row 1: Knit across.

Row 2 (Right side)**:** Knit increase *(Figs. 6a & b, page 43)*, K4, [slip 1 as if to **knit**, K2 tog, PSSO *(Figs. 12a & b, page 45)*], K4, ★ knit increase twice, K4, slip 1 as if to **knit**, K2 tog, PSSO, K4; repeat from ★ across to last st, knit increase.

Row 3: Purl across.

Row 4: Repeat Row 2.

Row 5: Knit across; cut yarn.

Row 6: With next color, repeat Row 2.

Row 7: Purl across.

Row 8: Repeat Row 2.

Row 9: Purl across.

Row 10: Purl increase *(Fig. 7, page 44)*, P4, P3 tog *(Fig. 15, page 46)*, P4, ★ purl increase twice, P4, P3 tog, P4; repeat from ★ across to last st, purl increase; cut yarn.

Row 11: With next color, purl across.

Repeat Rows 2-11 for pattern until piece measures approximately 50" (127 cm) from cast on edge, ending by working 5 rows of Green.

Bind off all sts in **knit**.

"Cedar Cove has changed in some ways, but it's stayed the same in others," Charlotte said. "A lot of people around here are employed by the Bremerton shipyard, just like they were in the forties. Naturally the Navy has a real impact on the town's economy."

Tom jerkily put his right hand over his heart.

"You served in the military?" Charlotte asked.

The older man's nod was barely perceptible.

"God bless you," Charlotte said.

—from
16 Lighthouse Road

baby blanket

No matter how you arrive in Cedar Cove—by boat, train, automobile, or even by the proverbial stork—you're sure to get a warm welcome. Baby blankets are, perhaps, the most useful and lovingly crafted items that any knitter can make. This one is created in a medium blue, but would be darling in any color you choose.

● ● □ □ **EASY**

Finished Size: 33" x 37" (84 cm x 94 cm)

MATERIALS

Bulky Weight Yarn
    [3.5 ounces, 164 yards
      (100 grams, 150 meters) per ball]:
      5 balls
    29" (73.5 cm) or longer circular knitting
      needle, size 10 (6 mm) **or** size needed for
      gauge

GAUGE: In pattern, 2 repeats (16 sts)
      and 24 rows = 4³/₄" (12 cm)

Tip: A Seed Stitch border surrounds the check pattern. Seed Stitch is made by knitting the purl stitches and purling the knit stitches as they face you.

BLANKET
Cast on 111 sts.

Rows 1-18: K1, (P1, K1) across (Seed Stitch Border).

Row 19 (Right side)**:** (K1, P1) 6 times, K6, P3, (K5, P3) 9 times, K6, (P1, K1) 6 times.

Row 20: K1, (P1, K1) 6 times, P5, (K3, P5) 10 times, K1, (P1, K1) 6 times.

Row 21: (K1, P1) 6 times, K6, P1, YO *(Fig. 4b, page 43)*, P2 tog *(Fig. 13, page 45)*, (K5, P1, YO, P2 tog) 9 times, K6, (P1, K1) 6 times.

Row 22: K1, (P1, K1) 6 times, P5, (K3, P5) 10 times, K1, (P1, K1) 6 times.

Row 23: (K1, P1) 6 times, K6, P3, (K5, P3) 9 times, K6, (P1, K1) 6 times.

Row 24: K1, (P1, K1) 6 times, P5, (K3, P5) 10 times, K1, (P1, K1) 6 times.

Row 25: (K1, P1) 6 times, K2, P3, (K5, P3) 10 times, K2, (P1, K1) 6 times.

Row 26: (K1, P1) 7 times, K3, (P5, K3) 10 times, (P1, K1) 7 times.

Row 27: (K1, P1) 6 times, K2, P1, YO, P2 tog, (K5, P1, YO, P2 tog) 10 times, K2, (P1, K1) 6 times.

Row 28: (K1, P1) 7 times, K3, (P5, K3) 10 times, (P1, K1) 7 times.

Row 29: (K1, P1) 6 times, K2, P3, (K5, P3) 10 times, K2, (P1, K1) 6 times.

Row 30: (K1, P1) 7 times, K3, (P5, K3) 10 times, (P1, K1) 7 times.

Repeat Rows 19-30 for pattern until Blanket measures approximately 33¹/₂" (85 cm) from cast on edge, ending by working Row 24 or Row 30.

Repeat Rows 1-18 for Seed Stitch Border.

Bind off all sts in pattern.

Design by Bonita Dubil.

Maryellen's baby could be born at any time, and she'd never looked forward to anything more. She was ready. Her bag was packed, the house was clean, and her baby blanket was finished. She'd bring the baby home from the hospital wrapped in the blanket she'd knit herself.
—from
6 Rainier Drive

puget sound afghan

To create a lacy and feminine throw that still offers plenty of warmth, try this pattern. The double thickness of yarn gives it substance, while the fluffy texture of the yarn keeps the fabric from becoming too heavy. The Senior Center knitters have made this afghan in almost every color imaginable, but they all agree that this soft teal hue is soothing to the eye.

◼◼◼◻ INTERMEDIATE

Finished Size: 46" x 61" (117 cm x 155 cm)

MATERIALS
Medium Weight Yarn **MEDIUM 4**
  [6 ounces, 278 yards
    (170 grams, 254 meters) per skein]:
    8 skeins
29" (73.5 cm) or longer circular knitting
  needle, size 15 (10 mm) **or** size needed for
  gauge

Hold two strands of yarn together throughout for a thick and lacy afghan that will be warm and also pretty.

GAUGE: In Seed Stitch,
      11 sts and 18 rows = 4" (10 cm)

Tip: A Seed Stitch border surrounds the lace panels. Seed Stitch is made by knitting the purl stitches and purling the knit stitches as they face you.

Gauge Swatch: 4" (10 cm) square
Cast on 11 sts.
Rows 1-18: K1, (P1, K1) across.
Bind off.

AFGHAN
Cast on 126 sts.

Row 1: (K1, P1) across.

Row 2 (Right side)**:** (P1, K1) across.

Rows 3-9: Repeat Rows 1 and 2, 3 times; then repeat Row 1 once **more** (Seed Stitch Border).

Row 10: (P1, K1) 3 times, P2, K2, YO *(Fig. 4a, page 43)*, K3 tog *(Fig. 10, page 44)*, YO, K2, (P1, K2, YO, K3 tog, YO, K2) twice, ★ P2, (K1, P1) twice, K2, YO, K3 tog, YO, K2, (P1, K2, YO, K3 tog, YO, K2) twice; repeat from ★ 2 times **more**, (P1, K1) 4 times.

Row 11: (K1, P1) 3 times, K2, P7, (K1, P7) twice, ★ K2, (P1, K1) twice, P7, (K1, P7) twice; repeat from ★ 2 times **more**, (K1, P1) 4 times.

Row 12: (P1, K1) 3 times, P2, K2 tog *(Fig. 9, page 44)*, YO, K3, YO, K2 tog, (P1, K2 tog, YO, K3, YO, K2 tog) twice, ★ P2, (K1, P1) twice, K2 tog, YO, K3, YO, K2 tog, (P1, K2 tog, YO, K3, YO, K2 tog) twice; repeat from ★ 2 times **more**, (P1, K1) 4 times.

Row 13: (K1, P1) 3 times, K2, P7, (K1, P7) twice, ★ K2, (P1, K1) twice, P7, (K1, P7) twice; repeat from ★ 2 times **more**, (K1, P1) 4 times.

Repeat Rows 10-13 for pattern until Afghan measures approximately 59" (150 cm) from cast on edge, ending by working Row 10 or Row 12.

Last 9 Rows (Seed Stitch Border)**:** Repeat Rows 1-9.

Bind off all sts in pattern.

Design by Lee Tribett.

Evelyn was almost finished with the afghan she was knitting for her daughter. The pattern was a lovely one and it had already been completed by several others in the group.

—from
16 Lighthouse Road

a spot for pets

This medium-size pet bed is just like the one that Charlotte knitted for her "guard cat," Harry. Grace Sherman has been hinting that Charlotte should make more pet beds in varying sizes, then sell them to help the humane society. Charlotte has figured out that Grace wants to buy a large bed for Buttercup, her golden retriever. But what Grace doesn't know is that Charlotte is already working on a bed for Buttercup's birthday.

■■☐☐☐ EASY

Size	Finished Measurement
Small	23" (58.5 cm) square
Medium	29" (73.5 cm) square
Large	34$^{1}/_{2}$" (87.5 cm) square

Note: Instructions are written for size Small, with sizes Medium and Large in braces { }. Instructions will be easier to read if you circle all the numbers pertaining to your pet's size. If only one number is given, it applies to all sizes.

MATERIALS

Super Bulky Weight Yarn 🄺
[6 ounces, 143 yards
(170 grams, 130 meters) per skein]:
Red - 3 skeins
Tan - 3 skeins
Straight knitting needles, size 13 (9 mm) **or**
size needed for gauge
Markers
Batting
Yarn needle

GAUGE: In Stockinette Stitch,
10 sts and 14 rows = 4" (10 cm)

FRONT

With Tan, cast on 58{72-86} sts.

Work in Stockinette Stitch (knit one row, purl one row) for 2$^{3}/_{4}${5$^{3}/_{4}$-8$^{1}/_{2}$}"/7{14.5-21.5} cm, ending by working a **purl** row.

Next Row: K7{14-21}, place marker *(see Markers, page 42)*, follow chart across 44 sts, page 29, working spot with Red *(Fig. 2, page 29)*, place marker, K7{14-21}.

Work even following chart between markers.

Work in Stockinette Stitch for 2$^{3}/_{4}${5$^{3}/_{4}$-8$^{1}/_{2}$}"/7{14.5-21.5} cm, ending by working a **purl** row.

Bind off all sts in **knit**.

BACK

Work same as Front, reversing colors.

ASSEMBLY

Sew Front and Back together, inserting desired layers of batting before closing.

If desired, tack batting to bed at center and corners, sewing through all layers to secure.

Design by Peggy Schultz.

G race woke early on Monday morning. Buttercup, her golden retriever, who slept on the floor beside her, got to her feet, tail waving vigorously as Grace folded back the covers and climbed out of bed.

"Good morning, sweetheart," Grace said, reaching for her robe. She wondered what Dan would think if he learned she'd replaced him with a dog.

—from *204 Rosewood Lane*

Jolene's pullover

Rachel Pendergast is a manicurist at the Get Nailed salon. Rachel doesn't knit, but she thought it would be nice to give a handmade sweater to her nine-year-old friend, Jolene Peyton. The little girl's mother died several years ago, and she looks upon Rachel as a substitute mom—or perhaps not a substitute at all! Rachel purchased the yarn for this pullover and promised one of her clients a series of free manicures if she would knit it for Jolene.

■■■□ INTERMEDIATE

Size	Actual Chest Measurement	Finished Chest Measurement
Small	26-28"/66-71 cm	30½" (77.5 cm)
Medium	29-31"/73.5-78.5 cm	33¼" (84.5 cm)
Large	32-34"/81.5-86.5 cm	36" (91.5 cm)

Note: Instructions are written for size Small, with sizes Medium and Large in braces { }. Instructions will be easier to read if you circle all the numbers pertaining to your child's size. If only one number is given, it applies to all sizes.

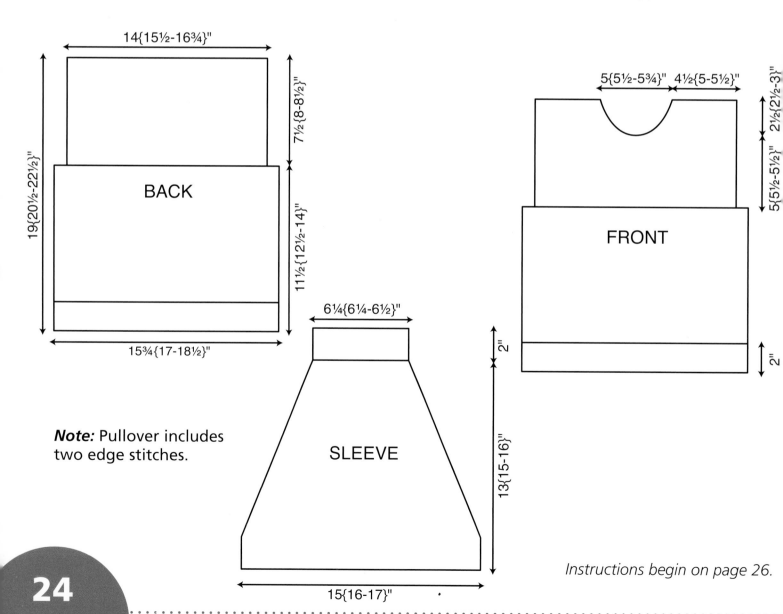

BACK

14{15½-16¾}"

7½{8-8½}"

19{20½-22½}"

11½{12½-14}"

15¾{17-18½}"

SLEEVE

6¼{6¼-6½}"

13{15-16}"

15{16-17}"

FRONT

5{5½-5¾}"   4½{5-5½}"

2½{2½-3}"

5{5½-5½}"

2"

2"

Note: Pullover includes two edge stitches.

Instructions begin on page 26.

24

"Daddy," Jolene said, "I like Rachel."

"Who's Rachel?" Bruce asked.

"Daddy! The lady who cut my hair."

"That's nice," Bruce replied absently.

Jolene nodded. "She wants a husband. I heard her talking to the lady next to her, and she said she wants to be married before she's thirty. I think you should marry her, Daddy."

"What?"

"You should marry Rachel," she repeated, as if that was a perfectly reasonable statement.

—from
311 Pelican Court

MATERIALS

Medium Weight Yarn 🧶 4

[6 ounces, 315 yards
(170 grams, 288 meters) per skein]:
3 skeins
Straight knitting needles, sizes 7 (4.5 mm)
and 9 (5.5 mm) **or** sizes needed for gauge
16" (40.5 cm) Circular knitting needle,
size 7 (4.5 mm)
Cable needle
Stitch holders - 2
Marker
Yarn needle

GAUGE: With larger size needles,
in Stockinette Stitch,
18 sts and 24 rows = 4" (10 cm)

Tip: Do not hesitate to change needle size to obtain correct gauge.

STITCH GUIDE

BACK CABLE (uses 4 sts)
Slip next 2 sts onto cable needle and hold in **back** of work, K2 from left needle, K2 from cable needle.
FRONT CABLE (uses 4 sts)
Slip next 2 sts onto cable needle and hold in **front** of work, K2 from left needle, K2 from cable needle.

BACK
RIBBING

With smaller size needles, cast on 70{76-82} sts.

Work in K1, P1 ribbing for 2" (5 cm) increasing one st at end of last row (*Fig. 7, page 44*): 71{77-83} sts.

BODY

Change to larger size needles.

Row 1 (Right side): Knit across.

Row 2: Purl across.

Row 3: K2, P1, (K5, P1) across to last 2 sts, K2.

Row 4: (P1, K1) twice, P3, (K1, P1, K1, P3) across to last 4 sts, (K1, P1) twice.

Row 5: K4, P1, K1, P1, (K3, P1, K1, P1) across to last 4 sts, K4.

Row 6: P5, (K1, P5) across.

Row 7: Knit across.

Row 8: Purl across.

Rows 9-11: Knit across.

Row 12: P2, K1, (P5, K1) across to last 2 sts, P2.

Rows 13 and 14: Repeat Rows 11 and 12.

Rows 15-17: Knit across.

Repeat Rows 2-17 until Back measures approximately 11$\frac{1}{2}${12$\frac{1}{2}$-14}"/29{32-35.5} cm from cast on edge, ending by working Row 8 or Row 14.

YOKE & ARMHOLE SHAPING

Rows 1 and 2: Bind off 4 sts, knit across: 63{69-75} sts.

Row 3: K 31{34-37}, knit into front **and** back of next st (*Figs. 6a & b, page 43*), knit across: 64{70-76} sts.

Row 4: Knit across.

Row 5: K8{10-12}, P1, K1, P1, K2, back cable, P1, K1, P1, ★ K6{7-8}, P1, K1, P1, K2, back cable, P1, K1, P1; repeat from ★ once **more**, K8{10-12}.

Row 6: P9{11-13}, K1, P8, K1, ★ P8{9-10}, K1, P8, K1; repeat from ★ once **more**, P9{11-13}.

Row 7: K8{10-12}, P1, K1, P1, front cable, K2, P1, K1, P1, ★ K6{7-8}, P1, K1, P1, front cable, K2, P1, K1, P1; repeat from ★ once **more**, K8{10-12}.

Row 8: P9{11-13}, K1, P8, K1, ★ P8{9-10}, K1, P8, K1; repeat from ★ once **more**, P9{11-13}.

Repeat Rows 5-8 until Yoke measures approximately 7½{8-8½}"/19{20.5-21.5} cm, ending by working a **wrong** side row.

Bind off 21{23-25} sts, work across in established pattern until 22{24-26} sts are on right needle, then slip them onto st holder; bind off remaining sts; cut yarn.

FRONT

Work same as Back until Yoke measures approximately 5{5½-5½}"/12.5{14-14} cm, ending by working a **wrong** side row: 64{70-76} sts.

NECK SHAPING

Both sides of Neck are worked at the same time, using a separate yarn for **each** side. Maintain established pattern throughout.

Row 1: Work across 24{27-29} sts, K2 tog *(Fig. 9, page 44)*, slip next 12{12-14} sts onto st holder; with second yarn, SSK *(Figs. 11a-c, page 45)*, work across: 25{28-30} sts **each** side.

Row 2 (Decrease row)**:** Work across to within 2 sts of neck edge, P2 tog through back loops *(Fig. 14, page 45)*; with second yarn, P2 tog *(Fig. 13, page 45)*, work across: 24{27-29} sts **each** side.

Row 3 (Decrease row)**:** Work across to within 2 sts of neck edge, K2 tog; with second yarn, SSK, work across: 23{26-28} sts **each** side.

Row 4: Work across; with second yarn, work across.

Repeat Rows 3 and 4, 1{2-2} time(s); then repeat Row 3 once **more**: 21{23-25} sts **each** side.

Work even until Front measures same as Back, ending by working a **wrong** side row.

Bind off remaining sts.

Sew shoulder seams.

SLEEVE

With **right** side facing and using larger size needles, pick up 68{72-76} sts evenly spaced across Front and Back Yoke *(Fig. 16a, page 46)*.

Row 1: P7{7-8}, K1, P8, K1, ★ P 12{14-15}, K1, P8, K1; repeat from ★ once **more**, P7{7-8}.

Row 2: K6{6-7}, P1, K1, P1, front cable, K2, P1, K1, P1, ★ K 10{12-13}, P1, K1, P1, front cable, K2, P1, K1, P1; repeat from ★ once **more**, K6{6-7}.

Row 3: P7{7-8}, K1, P8, K1, ★ P 12{14-15}, K1, P8, K1; repeat from ★ once **more**, P7{7-8}.

Row 4: K6{6-7}, P1, K1, P1, K2, back cable, P1, K1, P1, ★ K 10{12-13}, P1, K1, P1, K2, back cable, P1, K1, P1; repeat from ★ once **more**, K6{6-7}.

Rows 5-13: Repeat Rows 1-4 twice, then repeat Row 1 once **more**.

Row 14 (Decrease row)**:** K1, SSK, K3{3-4}, P1, K1, P1, front cable, K2, P1, K1, P1, ★ K 10{12-13}, P1, K1, P1, front cable, K2, P1, K1, P1; repeat from ★ once **more**, K3{3-4}, K2 tog, K1: 66{70-74} sts.

Row 15: P6{6-7}, K1, P8, K1, ★ P 12{14-15}, K1, P8, K1; repeat from ★ once **more**, P6{6-7}.

Row 16: K5{5-6}, P1, K1, P1, K2, back cable, P1, K1, P1, ★ K 10{12-13}, P1, K1, P1, K2, back cable, P1, K1, P1; repeat from ★ once **more**, K5{5-6}.

Row 17: P6{6-7}, K1, P8, K1, ★ P 12{14-15}, K1, P8, K1; repeat from ★ once **more**, P6{6-7}.

Row 18 (Decrease row)**:** K1, SSK, K2{2-3}, P1, K1, P1, front cable, K2, P1, K1, P1, ★ K 10{12-13}, P1, K1, P1, front cable, K2, P1, K1, P1; repeat from ★ once **more**, K2{2-3}, K2 tog, K1: 64{68-72} sts.

Row 19: P5{5-6}, K1, P8, K1, ★ P 12{14-15}, K1, P8, K1; repeat from ★ once **more**, P5{5-6}.

Instructions continued on page 28.

Row 20: K4{4-5}, P1, K1, P1, K2, back cable, P1, K1, P1, ★ K 10{12-13}, P1, K1, P1, K2, back cable, P1, K1, P1; repeat from ★ once **more**, K4{4-5}.

Row 21: P5{5-6}, K1, P8, K1, ★ P 12{14-15}, K1, P8, K1; repeat from ★ once **more**, P5{5-6}.

Row 22 (Decrease row): K1, SSK, K1{1-2}, P1, K1, P1, front cable, K2, P1, K1, P1, ★ K 10{12-13}, P1, K1, P1, front cable, K2, P1, K1, P1; repeat from ★ once **more**, K1{1-2}, K2 tog, K1: 62{66-70} sts.

Row 23: P4{4-5}, K1, P8, K1, ★ P 12{14-15}, K1, P8, K1; repeat from ★ once **more**, P4{4-5}.

Row 24: K3{3-4}, P1, K1, P1, K2, back cable, P1, K1, P1, ★ K 10{12-13}, P1, K1, P1, K2, back cable, P1, K1, P1; repeat from ★ once **more**, K3{3-4}.

Row 25: P4{4-5}, K1, P8, K1, ★ P 12{14-15}, K1, P8, K1; repeat from ★ once **more**, P4{4-5}.

Row 26 (Decrease row): K1, SSK, knit across to last 3 sts, K2 tog, K1: 60{64-68} sts.

Rows 27-29: Knit across.

Row 30 (Decrease row): K1, SSK, knit across to last 3 sts, K2 tog, K1: 58{62-66} sts.

Row 31: Purl across.

Row 32: K5{4-6}, P1, (K5, P1) across to last 4{3-5} sts, knit across.

Row 33: P3{2-4}, K1, P1, K1, (P3, K1, P1, K1) across to last 4{3-5} sts, purl across.

Row 34 (Decrease row): K1, SSK, K 0{0-1} **(see Zeros, page 42)**, P1{0-1}, (K3, P1, K1, P1) across to last 6{5-7} sts, K3{2-3}, P 0{0-1}, K2 tog, K1: 56{60-64} sts.

Row 35: P6{5-7}, K1, (P5, K1) across to last 1{6-2} sts, purl across.

Row 36: Knit across.

Row 37: Purl across.

Row 38 (Decrease row): K1, SSK, knit across to last 3 sts, K2 tog, K1: 54{58-62} sts.

Rows 39 and 40: Knit across.

Row 41: P2{1-3}, K1, (P5, K1) across to last 3{2-4} sts, purl across.

Row 42 (Decrease row): K1, SSK, knit across to last 3 sts, K2 tog, K1: 52{56-60} sts.

Row 43: P1{6-2}, K1, (P5, K1) across to last 2{1-3} sts, purl across.

Rows 44 and 45: Knit across.

Row 46 (Decrease row): K1, SSK, knit across to last 3 sts, K2 tog, K1: 50{54-58} sts.

Working in pattern, continue to decrease one stitch at **each** edge in same manner, every fourth row, 6{9-10} times **more**: 38{36-38} sts.

Work even until Sleeve measures approximately 13{15-16}"/33{38-40.5} cm, ending by working a **wrong** side row.

RIBBING
Change to smaller size needles.

Row 1: Work in K1, P1 ribbing across decreasing 10{8-8} sts evenly spaced: 28{28-30} sts.

Work in established ribbing for 2" (5 cm), ending by working a **wrong** side row.

Bind off all sts **loosely** in ribbing.

Repeat for second Sleeve.

FINISHING
Weave underarm and side in one continuous seam **(Fig. 18, page 46)**.

NECK BAND

With **right** side facing and using circular needle, knit 22{24-26} sts from Back st holder, pick up 15{15-18} sts along left Front neck edge, slip 12{12-14} sts from Front st holder onto second end of circular needle and knit across, pick up 15{15-18} sts along right Front neck edge, place marker to indicate beginning of round **(see Markers, page 42)**: 64{66-76} sts.

Work in K1, P1 ribbing for 2" (5 cm).

Bind off all sts **very loosely** in established ribbing.

Fold Neck Band in half to wrong side of sweater and sew loosely in place along base of ribbing.

Design by Joan Beebe.

....

a spot for pets
continued

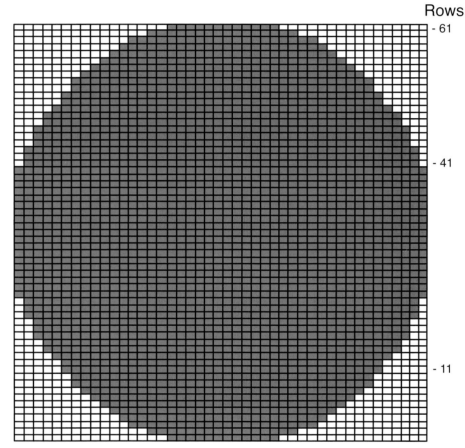

Rows
- 61
- 41
- 11

CHANGING COLORS

Use a separate ball of yarn for each section of color. Do not carry unused yarn across the back of the work. When changing colors, always pick up the new color yarn from beneath the dropped yarn and keep the color which has just been worked to the left **(Fig. 2)**. This will join the sections together.

Fig. 2

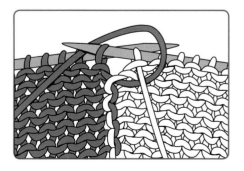

Leif's sweater

This pattern is one that caught Charlotte's eye. She's looking forward to using the very same yarn color to knit it for her little great-grandson, Leif Gunderson, who is absolutely adorable in blue. Charlotte's planning to get started on it right after she finishes the man's sweater that's currently taking up her time. Then again, perhaps it's the mystery man himself who actually has her so preoccupied.

◼◼◼◻ **INTERMEDIATE**

Size	Actual Chest Measurement	Finished Chest Measurement
Small	22-24½"/56-62 cm	26½" (67.5 cm)
Medium	25-27"/63.5-68.5 cm	29" (73.5 cm)
Large	27½-29"/70-73.5 cm	31¼" (79.5 cm)

Note: Instructions are written for size Small, with sizes Medium and Large in braces { }. Instructions will be easier to read if you circle all the numbers pertaining to your child's size. If only one number is given, it applies to all sizes.

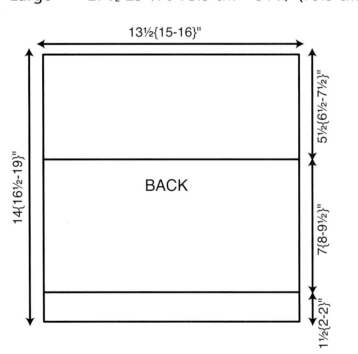

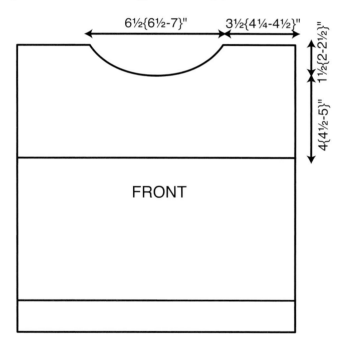

Note: Sweater includes two edge stitches.

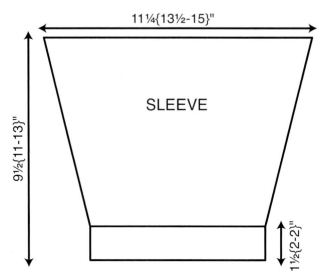

Instructions begin on page 32.

Charlotte sat with her feet up in front of the fireplace, knitting what seemed to be a man's sweater, although she hadn't said who it was for.

—from
311 Pelican Court

MATERIALS

Light Weight Superwash Wool Yarn **LIGHT 3**
  [4 ounces, 240 yards
    (113 grams, 220 meters) per hank]:
    3{3-4} hanks
Two 29" (73.5 cm) Circular knitting needles,
  size 6 (4 mm) **or** size needed for gauge
Note: A pair of straight knitting needles can
be substituted for one of the circular knitting
needles which is used to work the 3-needle
bind off.
16" (40.5 cm) Circular knitting needle,
  size 4 (3.5 mm)
Stitch holders - 2
Marker
Yarn needle

GAUGE: With larger size needles,
      in Seed Stitch, 20 sts = 4" (10 cm);
      in Basket Weave,
      5 repeats (30 sts) = 6" (15.25 cm);
      24 rows = 3" (7.5 cm)

Tip: Do not hesitate to change needle size to obtain correct gauge.

BACK
RIBBING

With smaller size needle, cast on 66{74-78} sts.

Row 1: P2, (K2, P2) across.

Row 2: K2, (P2, K2) across.

Repeat Rows 1 and 2 for 1½{2-2}"/4{5-5} cm, ending by working Row 1 and increasing 1{0-1} st(s) at **each** edge of last row *(see Zeros, page 42, or Figs. 6a & b, page 43)*: 68{74-80} sts.

BODY

Change to larger size needles.

Row 1 (Right side): Knit across.

Row 2: P3, K4, (P2, K4) across to last st, P1.

Rows 3 and 4: Repeat Rows 1 and 2.

Row 5: Knit across.

Row 6: (K4, P2) across to last 2 sts, K2.

Rows 7 and 8: Repeat Rows 5 and 6.

Repeat Rows 1-8 for Basket Weave until Back measures approximately 8½{10-11½}"/21.5{25.5-29} cm from cast on edge, ending by working Row 4 or Row 8.

YOKE

Rows 1 and 2: Knit across.

Rows 3 and 4: Purl across.

Rows 5-8: Repeat Rows 1-4.

Row 9: (K1, P1) across.

Row 10: (P1, K1) across.

Repeat Rows 9 and 10 for Seed Stitch until Yoke measures approximately 5½{6½-7½}"/14{16.5-19} cm, ending by working a **wrong** side row; cut yarn.

Leave stitches on the circular needle and set Back aside.

FRONT

Work same as Back until Yoke measures approximately 4{4½-5}"/10{11.5-12.5} cm, ending by working a **wrong** side row: 68{74-80} sts.

NECK SHAPING

Both sides of Neck are worked at the same time, using a separate yarn for **each** side. Maintain established pattern throughout.

Row 1: Work across 23{26-28} sts, slip next 22{22-24} sts onto st holder; with second yarn, work across: 23{26-28} sts **each** side.

Row 2 (Decrease row): Work across to within 2 sts of neck edge, decrease *(see Decreases, pages 44 and 45)*; with second yarn, decrease, work across: 22{25-27} sts **each** side.

Row 3: Work across; with second yarn, work across.

Rows 4-10: Repeat Rows 2 and 3, 3 times; then repeat Row 2 once **more**: 18{21-23} sts **each** side.

Work even until Front measures same as Back, ending by working a **wrong** side row.

Join Front to Back at Left shoulder using the 3-needle bind off method as follows: Holding pieces with **right** sides together and needles parallel to each other, insert a third needle as if to **knit** into the first st on the front needle **and** into the first st on the back needle **(Fig. 3)**. Knit these 2 sts tog and slip them off the needle, ★ knit the next st on each needle tog and slip them off the needle. To bind off, insert the left needle into the first st on the right needle and pull the first st over the second st and off the right needle; repeat from ★ across until all of the sts on the shoulder have been bound off.

Fig. 3

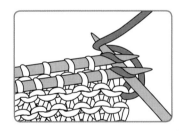

Slip 32{32-34} sts from Back onto st holder for neck. Join Front to Back at Right shoulder using the 3-needle bind off method.

SLEEVE (Make 2)
RIBBING
With smaller size needle, cast on 38{42-42} sts **loosely**.

Row 1: P2, (K2, P2) across.

Row 2: K2, (P2, K2) across.

Repeat Rows 1 and 2 for 1½{2-2}"/4{5-5} cm, ending by working Row 1.

BODY
Change to larger size needles.

Row 1 (Right side)**:** Knit across increasing 6{8-8} sts evenly spaced **(see Increases, pages 43 and 44)**: 44{50-50} sts.

Beginning with Row 2, work in Basket Weave same as Back, increasing one stitch at **each** edge, every 8{6-6} rows, 6{9-12} times: 56{68-74} sts.

Work even until Sleeve measures approximately 9½{11-13}"/24{28-33} cm from cast on edge **or to desired length**, ending by working a **wrong** side row.

Bind off all sts in pattern.

FINISHING
Sew Sleeves to sweater, placing center of Sleeve at shoulder seam and beginning between Garter ridge (Rows 4 and 5) at beginning of Yoke.

Weave underarm and side in one continuous seam **(Fig. 18, page 46)**.

NECK RIBBING
With **right** side facing, slip 32{32-34} sts from Back st holder onto smaller size needle and knit across, pick up 11{15-19} sts evenly spaced along left Front neck edge **(Fig. 16a, page 46)**, slip 22{22-24} sts from Front st holder onto second end of circular needle and knit across, pick up 11{15-19} sts evenly spaced along right Front neck edge, place marker to indicate beginning of round **(see Markers, page 42)**: 76{84-96} sts.

Work in K2, P2 ribbing for 1½" (4 cm).

Bind off all sts **loosely** in established ribbing.

Design by Terri Fahrenholtz.

cedar Cove cooks!

If you haven't visited *DebbieMacomber.com*, you're missing a treat! Debbie has invited her readers to contribute their favorite recipes, and you'll find dozens of delicious dishes on her Web site.

Just for fun, we're giving you four recipes here. Each has been "assigned" by Debbie to a favorite Cedar Cove character. What a nice way to keep the stories going while the author is hard at work on her next book!

shrimp enchiladas

Vegetable cooking spray

1 container (15 ounces) ricotta cheese

2 cups (8 ounces) shredded Monterey Jack cheese

1 pound small salad shrimp, cooked, shelled, and deveined

1 bunch green onions, chopped

$^1/_2$ cup cilantro leaves, chopped

Salt and pepper to taste

8 small flour tortillas

Red chile sauce

Tomatillo sauce or other green sauce

Preheat oven to 350°. Spray a 9 x 13-inch glass baking dish with cooking spray.

In a bowl, combine cheeses; stir in shrimp, onions, cilantro, salt and pepper. Spread mixture evenly on eight tortillas; roll up and place seam side down in baking dish. Alternating red and green sauces, stripe tops of tortillas with sauces.

Cover with foil and bake for 20 to 30 minutes or until hot. Use remaining sauces to decorate serving plates and to serve at the table.

yield: 8 enchiladas

I thought I would drop you a quick line to share Justine's recipe for shrimp enchiladas. It's a fast dish to put together, and perfect after a busy day at court!

— *Olivia Lockhart, Kitsap County Courthouse*

blueberry **muffins**

1³/₄ cups all-purpose flour

²/₃ cup sugar

1 tablespoon baking powder

³/₄ teaspoon salt

6 tablespoons butter or margarine

¹/₂ cup milk

1 egg

1 teaspoon grated lemon peel

¹/₂ teaspoon vanilla extract

1 cup fresh or frozen blueberries

I have several recipes that are favorites, but this one is a tradition at our B and B. I hope you enjoy my blueberry muffins.
— *Peggy Beldon, Thyme and Tide Bed and Breakfast*

Preheat oven to 400°.
Grease six muffin cups or line with paper cup liners.

In a medium bowl, combine flour, sugar, baking powder, and salt. Using a pastry blender, cut butter into dry ingredients until mixture resembles fine crumbs.

In a small bowl, beat milk, egg, lemon peel, and vanilla extract until blended. Add milk mixture to dry ingredients; stir just until moistened (batter will be lumpy). Fold in blueberries. Spoon batter into muffin cups.

Bake 20 to 25 minutes until tops are golden and a toothpick inserted in center of muffin comes out clean. Remove from pan; serve warm or at room temperature.

yield: 6 muffins

chocolate **zucchini** cake

1 cup vegetable oil

3 eggs

2 cups sugar

2 teaspoons vanilla extract

3 cups grated zucchini

2 $^1/_3$ cups all-purpose flour

$^1/_3$ cup unsweetened cocoa

2 teaspoons baking soda

1 teaspoon ground cinnamon
   (optional)

1 teaspoon salt

$^1/_4$ teaspoon baking powder

$^1/_2$ cup chopped nuts

$^1/_2$ cup chocolate chips

Preheat oven to 350°. Combine oil, eggs, sugar, vanilla, and zucchini in a bowl.

In a separate bowl, combine flour, cocoa, baking soda, cinnamon, salt, and baking powder. Add zucchini mixture to dry ingredients. Stir in nuts and chocolate chips. Pour into 2 greased 5 x 9-inch loaf pans.

Bake for 45 minutes or until a toothpick inserted in center of cake comes out clean. Cool on a wire rack and remove from pans.

yield: two 5 x 9-inch loaf cakes

The truth is, I don't cook much. But I am rather fond of zucchini and have a special recipe for chocolate zucchini cake that belonged to my grandmother. It's moist and a wonderful way to get in a veggie serving. (Although, to be perfectly honest, I feel like I'm cheating when the veggie comes in the form of a dessert!)

— *Rachel Pendergast, Get Nailed Salon*

clam
spaghetti

1/4 cup olive oil

2 to 3 red chili peppers or
    dried red pepper flakes to taste

1 large onion, chopped

3 to 5 garlic cloves, minced

1/2 cup chopped fresh basil or
    1 tablespoon dried

1 tablespoon dried oregano

1 teaspoon salt

1 teaspoon pepper

2 cans (4$\frac{1}{2}$ ounces each)
    chopped clams, liquid
    drained and reserved

1 package (16 ounces)
    fettuccine or spaghetti

1 cup chopped fresh parsley

The *secret*, I believe, to really good clam spaghetti is a cast-iron skillet. Over the years I've added scallops and shrimp to the clams, and it's even better. Experiment and see which seafood you like best.

— *Justine Gunderson*
The Lighthouse restaurant

Heat olive oil in cast-iron skillet over low heat. Add chili peppers, onion, and garlic. Cook about five minutes over low heat.

Add next 4 ingredients and liquid from clams. Continue to simmer about ten minutes.

Cook fettuccine or spaghetti according to package directions; drain.

Add clams and parsley to simmering mixture. Stir noodles into the sauce, tossing lightly. Serve immediately.

yield: 6 servings

thank you for helping
warm up
america!

Warm Up America! was started in 1991 by a Wisconsin yarn retailer named Evie Rosen. Evie decided to help the homeless by asking her customers, friends, and community to knit or crochet 7" x 9" blocks that would be joined into afghans. The efforts of those original contributors spread across the nation. To date, more than 80,000 afghans have been donated to victims of natural disasters, the homeless, shelters for battered women, and to many others who are in need.

You can also do much to help, and with so little effort. Debbie urges everyone who uses the patterns in this book to take a few minutes to knit a 7" x 9" block for this worthy cause. To help you get started, she's providing these four block patterns. Please take time to create a block for Warm Up America!, and ask your friends to get involved, as well.

If you are able to provide a completed afghan, Warm Up America! requests that you donate it directly to your local chapter of the American Red Cross or to any charity or social services agency in your community. If you require assistance in assembling the blocks into an afghan, please include your name and address inside the packaging and ship your 7" x 9" blocks to:

Warm Up America! Foundation
2500 Lowell Road
Ranlo, NC 28054

Remember, just a little bit of yarn can make a big difference to someone in need!

Basic patchwork afghans are made of forty-nine 7" x 9" (18 cm x 23 cm) rectangular blocks that are sewn together. Any pattern stitch can be used for the rectangle. Use acrylic medium weight yarn and size 8 (5 mm) straight knitting needles or size needed to obtain the gauge of 9 stitches to 2" (5 cm).

CHECKERBOARD BLOCK
Multiple of 6 sts.

Cast on 30 sts.

Rows 1-3: (P3, K3) across.

Rows 4-6: (K3, P3) across.

Repeat Rows 1-6 for pattern until Block measures approximately 9" (23 cm) from cast on edge, ending by working Row 3 or Row 6.

Bind off all sts in pattern.

CROCUS BUDS BLOCK
Multiple of 2 sts + 1.

Cast on 31 sts.

Row 1 (Right side)**:** K1, (YO, K2) across *(Fig. 4a, page 43)*.

Row 2: P4, with left needle bring the third st on right needle over the first 2 sts and off the needle, ★ P3, with left needle bring the third st on right needle over the first 2 sts and off the needle; repeat from ★ across.

Row 3: (K2, YO) across to last st, K1.

Row 4: ★ P3, with left needle bring the third st on right needle over the first 2 sts and off the needle; repeat from ★ across to last st, P1.

Repeat Rows 1-4 for pattern until Block measures approximately 9" (23 cm) from cast on edge, ending by working Row 2 or Row 4.

Bind off all sts in knit.

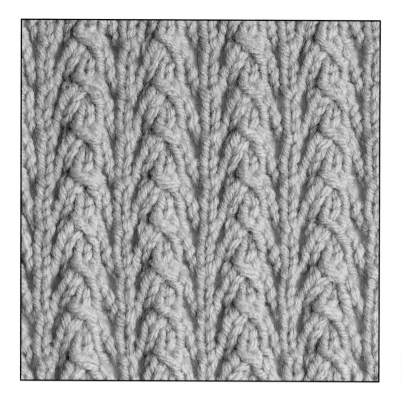

LITTLE FOUNTAIN BLOCK

Multiple of 4 sts + 1.

Cast on 33 sts.

Row 1 (Right side): K1, (YO, K3, YO, K1) across *(Fig. 4a, page 43)*.

Row 2: Purl across.

Row 3: K2, [slip 1 as if to **knit**, K2 tog, PSSO *(Figs. 12a & b, page 45)*]; ★ K3, slip 1 as if to **knit**, K2 tog, PSSO; repeat from ★ across to last 2 sts, K2.

Row 4: Purl across.

Repeat Rows 1-4 for pattern until Block measures approximately 9" (23 cm) from cast on edge, ending by working Row 4.

Bind off all sts in knit.

CABLE & BOBBLES BLOCK

Additional materials: cable needle

Cast on 33 sts.

Row 1 (Right side): P 14, slip next 3 sts onto cable needle and hold in **back** of work, K2 from left needle, K3 from cable needle, purl across.

Row 2: K 14, P5, K 14.

Row 3: P 14, K5, P 14.

Row 4: K 14, P5, K 14.

Row 5: P 14, K2, (K, P, K, P, K) all in next st, pass second, third, fourth, and fifth sts on right needle over first st, K2, P 14.

Row 6: K 14, P5, K 14.

Row 7: P 14, K5, P 14.

Row 8: K 14, P5, K 14.

Repeat Rows 1-8 for pattern until Block measures approximately 9" (23 cm) from cast on edge, ending by working Row 1.

Bind off all sts in pattern.

ABBREVIATIONS

cm	centimeters
K	knit
mm	millimeters
P	purl
PSSO	pass slipped stitch over
SSK	slip, slip, knit
st(s)	stitch(es)
tog	together
YO	yarn over

★ — work instructions following ★ as many **more** times as indicated in addition to the first time.

( ) or [ ] — work enclosed instructions **as many** times as specified by the number immediately following **or** work all enclosed instructions in the stitch indicated **or** contains explanatory remarks.

Colon (:) — the number given after a colon at the end of a row or round denotes the number of stitches you should have on that row or round.

Work even — work without increasing or decreasing in the established pattern.

GAUGE

Exact gauge is **essential** for proper size. Before beginning your project, make a sample swatch in the yarn and needle specified in the individual instructions. After completing the swatch, measure it, counting your stitches and rows carefully. If your swatch is larger or smaller than specified, **make another, changing needle size to get the correct gauge**. Keep trying until you find the size needles that will give you the specified gauge. Once proper gauge is obtained, measure width of project approximately every 3" (7.5 cm) to be sure gauge remains consistent.

HINTS

Good finishing techniques make a big difference in the quality of the piece. Always start a new ball at the beginning of a row, leaving ends long enough to weave in later. You can tie a loose knot close to the last stitch worked, but be sure to untie it before weaving in yarn ends.

Thread a yarn needle with the yarn end. With **wrong** side facing, weave the needle through several inches, then reverse the direction and weave it back through several inches. When the ends are secure, clip them off close to work.

KNIT TERMINOLOGY		
UNITED STATES		**INTERNATIONAL**
gauge	=	tension
bind off	=	cast off
yarn over (YO)	=	yarn forward (yfwd) **or** yarn around needle (yrn)

MARKERS

As a convenience to you, we have used markers to help distinguish the beginning of a pattern or a round. Place markers as instructed. You may use purchased markers or tie a length of contrasting color yarn around the needle. When you reach a marker on each row or round, slip it from the left needle to the right needle; remove it when no longer needed.

ZEROS

To consolidate the length of an involved pattern, Zeros are sometimes used so that all sizes can be combined. For example, K 0{0-1} means that the first two sizes would do nothing and the largest size would K1.

Yarn Weight Symbol & Names	SUPER FINE 1	FINE 2	LIGHT 3	MEDIUM 4	BULKY 5	SUPER BULKY 6
Type of Yarns in Category	Sock, Fingering Baby	Sport, Baby	DK, Light Worsted	Worsted, Afghan, Aran	Chunky, Craft, Rug	Bulky, Roving
Knit Gauge Ranges in Stockinette St to 4" (10 cm)	27-32 sts	23-26 sts	21-24 sts	16-20 sts	12-15 sts	6-11 sts
Advised Needle Size Range	1-3	3-5	5-7	7-9	9-11	11 and larger

SKILL LEVELS	
◖□□□ BEGINNER	Projects for first-time knitters using basic knit and purl stitches. Minimal shaping.
◖◗□□ EASY	Projects using basic stitches, repetitive stitch patterns, simple color changes, and simple shaping and finishing.
◖◗◗□ INTERMEDIATE	Projects with a variety of stitches, such as basic cables and lace, simple intarsia, double-pointed needles and knitting in the round needle techniques, mid-level shaping and finishing.
◖◗◗◗ EXPERIENCED	Projects using advanced techniques and stitches, such as short rows, fair isle, more intricate intarsia, cables, lace patterns, and numerous color changes.

KNITTING NEEDLES															
U.S.	0	1	2	3	4	5	6	7	8	9	10	10½	11	13	15	17
U.K.	13	12	11	10	9	8	7	6	5	4	3	2	1	00	000	---
Metric - mm	2	2.25	2.75	3.25	3.5	3.75	4	4.5	5	5.5	6	6.5	8	9	10	12.75

YARN OVERS

A yarn over **(abbreviated YO)** is simply placing the yarn over the right needle creating an extra stitch. Since the yarn over does produce a hole in the knit fabric, it is used for a lacy effect. On the row following a yarn over, you must be careful to keep it on the needle and treat it as a stitch by knitting or purling it as instructed.

To make a yarn over, you'll loop the yarn over the needle like you would to knit or purl a stitch, bringing it either to the front or the back of the piece so that it'll be ready to work the next stitch, creating a new stitch on the needle as follows:

Between Knit Stitches

Bring the yarn forward **between** the needles, then back **over** the top of the right hand needle, so that it is now in position to knit the next stitch **(Fig. 4a)**.

Fig. 4a

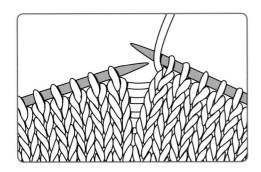

Between Purl Stitches

Take the yarn **over** the right hand needle to the back, then forward **between** the needles again, so that it is now in position to purl the next stitch **(Fig. 4b)**.

Fig. 4b

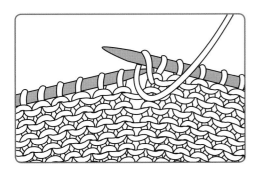

ADDING NEW STITCHES

Insert the right needle into the stitch as if to **knit**, yarn over and pull loop through **(Fig. 5a)**, insert left needle into loop just worked from front to back and slip it onto the left needle **(Fig. 5b)**. Repeat for required number of stitches.

Fig. 5a   **Fig. 5b**

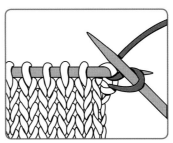   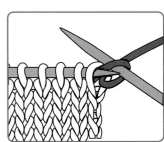

INCREASES

The increases in this book uses one stitch to make two stitches. You will have two stitches on the right needle for the one stitch worked off the left needle. The type of increase used depends on the stitch needed to maintain pattern.

KNIT INCREASE

Knit the next stitch but do not slip the old stitch off the left needle **(Fig. 6a)**. Insert the right needle into the **back** loop of the **same** stitch and knit it **(Fig. 6b)**, then slip the old stitch off the left needle.

Fig. 6a   **Fig. 6b**

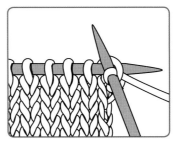   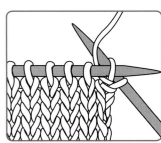

PURL INCREASE

Purl the next stitch but do not slip the old stitch off the left needle. Insert the right needle into the **back** loop of the **same** stitch **(Fig. 7)** and purl it, then slip the old stitch off the left needle.

Fig. 7

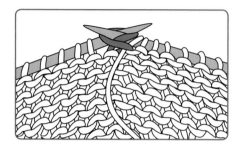

KNIT/PURL COMBINATION INCREASE

Knit the next stitch but do not slip the old stitch off the left needle. Bring the yarn to the front. Insert the right needle into the **front** loop of the **same** stitch **(Fig. 8)** and purl it, then slip the old stitch off the left needle.

Fig. 8

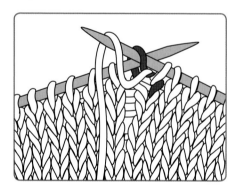

PURL/KNIT COMBINATION INCREASE

Purl the next stitch but do not slip the old stitch off the left needle. Bring the yarn to the back. Insert the right needle into the **front** loop of the **same** stitch and knit it, then slip the old stitch off the left needle.

INCREASING EVENLY

Add one to the number of increases required and divide that number into the number of stitches on the needle. Subtract one from the result and the new number is the approximate number of stitches to be worked between each increase. Adjust the number as needed.

DECREASES

KNIT 2 TOGETHER *(abbreviated K2 tog)*

Insert the right needle into the **front** of the first two stitches on the left needle as if to **knit** **(Fig. 9)**, then **knit** them together as if they were one stitch.

Fig. 9

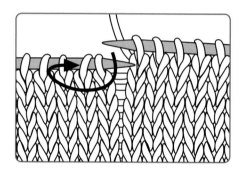

KNIT 3 TOGETHER *(abbreviated K3 tog)*

Insert the right needle into the **front** of the first three stitches on the left needle as if to **knit** **(Fig. 10)**, then **knit** them together as if they were one stitch.

Fig. 10

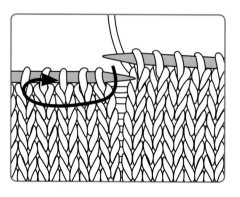

SLIP, SLIP, KNIT (abbreviated SSK)

With yarn in back of work, separately slip two stitches as if to **knit** (*Fig. 11a*). Insert the **left** needle into the **front** of both slipped stitches (*Fig. 11b*) and knit them together as if they were one stitch (*Fig. 11c*).

Fig. 11a

Fig. 11b

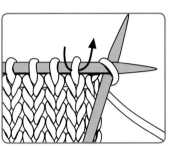

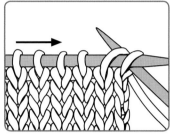

Fig. 11c

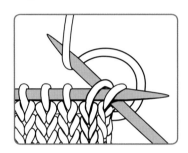

SLIP 1, KNIT 2 TOGETHER, PASS SLIPPED STITCH OVER (abbreviated slip 1, K2 tog, PSSO)

Slip one stitch as if to **knit** (*Fig. 12a*). Knit the next 2 stitches together (*Fig. 9, page 44*). With the left needle, bring the slipped stitch over the knit stitch (*Fig. 12b*) and off the needle.

Fig. 12a

Fig. 12b

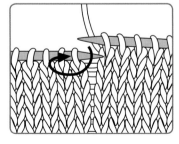

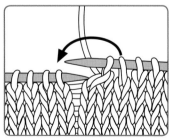

PURL 2 TOGETHER (abbreviated P2 tog)

Insert the right needle into the **front** of the first two stitches on the left needle as if to **purl** (*Fig. 13*), then **purl** them together as if they were one stitch.

Fig. 13

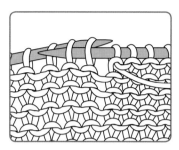

PURL 2 TOGETHER THROUGH BACK LOOP (abbreviated P2 tog through back loop)

Insert the right needle into the **back** of the second, then the first stitch on the left needle as if to **purl** (*Fig. 14*), then **purl** them together as if they were one stitch.

Fig. 14

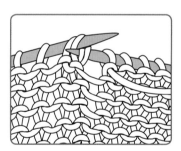

PURL 3 TOGETHER *(abbreviated P3 tog)*

Insert the right needle into the **front** of the first three stitches on the left needle as if to **purl** *(Fig. 15)*, then **purl** them together as if they were one stitch.

Fig. 15

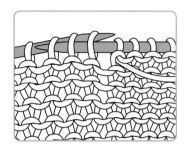

PICKING UP STITCHES

When instructed to pick up stitches, insert the needle from the **front** to the **back** under two strands at the edge of the worked piece *(Figs. 16 a & b)*. Put the yarn around the needle as if to **knit**, then bring the needle with the yarn back through the stitch to the right side, resulting in a stitch on the needle.
Repeat this along the edge, picking up the required number of stitches.
A crochet hook may be helpful to pull yarn through.

Fig. 16a

Fig. 16b

WHIPSTITCH

Sew through both pieces once to secure the beginning of the seam, leaving an ample yarn end to weave in later. Insert the needle from **front** to **back** through one strand on each piece *(Fig. 17)*. Bring the needle around and insert it from **front** to **back** through the next strand on both pieces.
Repeat along the edge.

Fig. 17

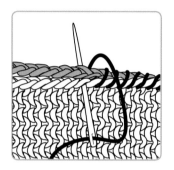

WEAVING SEAMS

With the **right** sides of both pieces facing you and edges even, sew through both pieces once to secure the beginning of the seam, leaving an ample yarn end to weave in later. Insert the needle under the bar **between** the first and second stitches on the row and pull the yarn through *(Fig. 18)*. Insert the needle under the next bar on the second side. Repeat from side to side, being careful to match rows. If the edges are different lengths, it may be necessary to insert the needle under two bars at one edge.

Fig. 18

FELTING

Machine Felting

Use ONLY a top-loading washer. Use the HOT wash setting with a COLD rinse cycle. DO NOT LET IT SPIN. This can cause creases that don't come out.

Our model was felted using 1 tablespoon of detergent. However, some don't like to use any soap or detergent at all.

Place your Knitted Tote in a tight-mesh sweater bag to contain the fuzz your Tote may shed. Check your project every 2-3 minutes to monitor for size and shrinkage. When you check your Tote, wear rubber gloves to protect your hands. Be careful, the water is very hot. If your Tote has not felted enough by the end of the wash cycle, repeat as needed and continue to check your Tote frequently.

If your Tote is left in the hot water too long, it can become too small and the fabric too tight. We do NOT recommend putting felted projects in the dryer. They will continue to shrink and shed and change their shape.

Blocking

Block IMMEDIATELY. Remove your Tote from the sweater bag and roll it in a towel and gently squeeze out the excess water. DO NOT WRING.

Form it into the size and shape you want by pulling and patting.

Place a plastic grocery bag inside out over plastic rigid foam board block. This is used to make it easier to pull the felted Tote over the block. Place the Tote over the end of the plastic rigid foam board and pull downward until the entire Tote is on the block. Place plastic wrap around the block if the felt will no longer slide.

Let your Tote air dry even though it may take several days.

yarn information

The projects in this leaflet were made using a variety of yarns. Any brand of yarn in the specified weight may be used. It is best to refer to the yardage/meters when determining how many balls or skeins to purchase. Remember, to arrive at the finished size and to achieve the same look, it is the GAUGE/TENSION that is important, not the brand of yarn.

For your convenience, listed below are the specific yarns used to create our photography models.

SCARF EXCHANGE
1. Solid Scarf
Caron® Charming
Red - #0005 Rich Red
2. Solid Scarf
Caron® Bliss
#0008 Sour Apple
3. Solid Scarf
Caron® Charming
#0007 Blue Green
4. Random Stripe Scarf
Caron® Bliss
Blue - #0011 Majestic
Red - #0003 Ruby Red
5. Even Stripe Scarf
Lion Brand® Homespun®
Red - #375 Candy Apple
Black - #373 Black
6. Even Stripe Scarf
Caron® Charming
Black Speckled - #0011 Jubilee
Red Speckled - #0005 Rich Red
7. Progressive Stripe Scarf
Lion Brand® Homespun®
Green - #389 Spring Green
Blue - #368 Montana Sky

CHARLOTTE'S KITCHEN COZIES
Lily® Sugar'n Cream®
Solid - #01742 Hot Blue
Multi - #02743 Summer Splash

CHEMO TURBAN
Lion Brand® Chenille Thick & Quick
#109 Royal Blue

FELTED KNITTING TOTE
Patons® Classic Wool, Merino
#00240 Leaf Green
#00202 Aran
#77732 That's Pink

TOM'S LAP ROBE
Lion Brand® Homespun®
Variegated - #395 Meadow
Gold - #394 Golden
Green - #123 Sea Spray

BABY BLANKET
Bernat® Softee® Chunky
#39132 Medium Blue

PUGET SOUND AFGHAN
Red Heart® Plush™
#9521 Lt Teal

A SPOT FOR PETS
Red Heart® Grandé™
Red - #2915 Cranberry
Tan - #2332 Linen

JOLENE'S PULLOVER
Caron® Simply Soft®
#9748 Rubine Red

LEIF'S SWEATER
Fancy Image Yarn DK
Machine Washable Merino Wool
#39132 Medium Blue